CLOSI ___ ,,, ,HE
KINGS HEAD

Poems of loss and loving

KARIN DE NOVELLIS
Illustration | Shelagh Atkinson
Design | Jeanne Pring

Karin De Novellis

First published in Great Britain by Karin De Novellis in 2022

Permission and enquiries:
Karin De Novellis
karindenovellis@gmail.com

Paperback
ISBN 978-1-7391413-0-1

This collection is dedicated to my husband, without whose daily struggle these poems would never have been written.

And to unpaid carers everywhere.

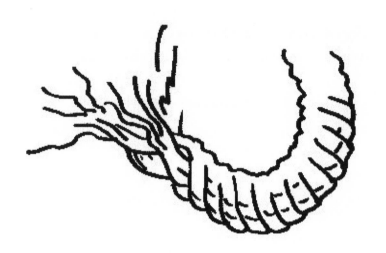

Thousands of clever thoughts skipping in my head.
One slipped up and lost its thread.
Dementia came along and dementia said,
"No more clever thoughts skipping in your head!"

Karin De Novellis

CONTENTS

Closing time at the Kings Head

Closing time at the Kings Head
and the public bar holds its locals tight.
Reluctant to leave, they know their rights
to stay and nurse their comfort tenderly.

He will be the very last to hoist his arse aloft,
balancing on rickety stool, the sway
of uncertain body and less certain mind,
stepping down gingerly lest
that tipple too many topples the lot.

Bumbling, unhurried, shuffling
across the familiar, uneven floor
towards the heavy oak door,
he has perfected the ounce of pull
to lift the latch and push.

A shock of damp air sneaks
through the crack, widening now
as he stumbles out into the cold mist,
disappearing like his thoughts.

Shoe which pinch

My mother taught me
to run barefoot, carefree
across Alpine meadows.
To relish the ooze of cowpat
squirming between my toes.

I learned to wear shoes
with an easy comfort.
Feet enclosed and safe
from worrisome weather.
An embalming of sorts.

But they have shrunk.
Stiffened leather wrinkled,
cracked and creaking,
stealing my freedom
to run, to fly.

I wear shoes which pinch,
crippling me before my time.

Dear Husband

Dear Husband, do stop fretting through the night.
It's hell to lie beside you and to hear
your gasping breath, as if in mortal fight
with double crossing monsters whom you fear.

You twist and turn, take up and fling aside
the bedclothes in an effort to be free,
then turn towards me arms out, stretching wide,
a man adrift upon his stormy sea.

I try to help, I really do my best
to soothe the frightful chaos in your head
which drives your body on some pointless quest
and tips you into feeling so much dread.

My words, my touch, my love all go unheeded.
I'm lost, confused; I don't have what is needed.

To take or not to take

They hand you a prescription and you take it on trust thinking it must be good, something to help. But you wonder how it might change you. For better or for worse? Will it forge connections or set landmines destroying my painful but oh so precious ways? Then the trust is broken. No, I won't do it. I'll hold on, treading the well-worn, bitter-sweet path. It's alright, I'll manage.

Then, I remember the one who lies beside me, breathing in and out as I breathe in and out. Who tosses and turns, when I wake tossing and turning at 3.00 a.m. in the morning with some dream still captive in my mind. Oh, the tales I bring her! I hold them fast, will not give up my thoughts, my understanding, my structure. Too much is slipping away.

She tries to soothe me, she really does. And I am petulant; will not concede, but sink into some state of false convenience which is not quite sleep, only to surge up again at 4.15, desperate, convinced as ever; I shall state my case – of which I'm certain!

She's getting angry now. I can feel it in the taut compassion of her voice. Yet still I insist, goading, beating the patience out of her until she buckles and cries out that she must sleep! Yes, of course. I'm repentant, a hint of fear in my apology.

For have I not asked once too often for her hand? Please, I beg you, give me your hand, sweet anchor that helps me know my otherness and binds me to myself. How can I manage without it? And so, we drift into uncertain sleep. I shall stay still, I shall no longer disturb, I have the hand and feel complete. I know my edges and now I lie, drifting away... No, I'm back at the institution which never ceases to demand my papers, to ask questions. Again I toss and in colder tone she chides, "What is it now?"

What can I say? I have no answer at 5.30 and will this night ever be done? It's the same, always the same and I have no idea what that is. She has no answer either. We are both lost in the polar wastes, ice fragmenting around us; no shore, only the hand. Give me your hand, please my angel. She does and we fall into waves of uneasy sleep, again and again until suddenly it's 7.30. "Put in your eye drops," she says, "and we can start the day."

And shall I do this every night? Shall I put her through this every night? Or shall I sell my soul to science for her sake, for the sake of sleep?

"I can't do this anymore," she says after three nights. "I can't carry on without sleep. It's time to try the pills. You might even feel better." She cajoles, tempts, persuades. No! I won't have it. "Not now," I say. And soft as a feather she is brushed away. "Alright, one more night."

Got it! One more night. I shall not wake. I'll be still as a lamb. I'll damn the institution; it can go to hell. I'll give up all hope of becoming a good and righteous man. I'll drift in the debris of my crumbling mind. I'll let go, lazily lose myself in blissful, untroubled sleep. I shall. Maybe...

Responsibility

I hold your world in my hand
like a blank sheet of paper.

I have the pattern of your days
etched like a map in my mind.

I know the words to soothe,
to remind you who you are.

Eyeing the door, my fingers
long to curl, crumple, hurl
the yoke, the weight; to escape.

Yet, immobile I sit and wait
for I hold your life
in the palm of my hand.

Spaghetti thoughts

HIM

Excuse me, can you help? I need to know where my wife is. She's supposed to meet me but she might not have the address you see and not know where to go. Sorry, can you remind me please, where am I now? 18 Silver Lane? Are you sure? Yes, that's my home. So, is that where I am?

I was worried about getting a bed for the night, have to make a booking you know. What? It's booked already, has been for months, then where am I sleeping? Here? Where's here again? 18 Silver Lane? Yes, that's my home and I've got to get a bed for tonight. I mean, where did I sleep last night? Here, really? Are you absolutely sure? Have you got documents to prove that? Because this address has nothing to do with my problem. Just a minute, sorry but who are you again?

HER

Oh no, here we go. I try and follow
as inner anguish squeezes bitter
sound into crackle glass of meaning.

Sliding slippery as spaghetti,
struggling to ride
the ride with you,

I fail and fall tumbled into irritation
while you go on and on and on...
I have to leave.

You stand there lost, confused,
bent, bereft and small.
I cannot bear it at all.

I try again, pick up my fork and
twist spaghetti thoughts
into a semblance of meaning.

HIM

Excuse me, where's my wife?
She might not know and
need reminding where to go

and with me out of sight
she might forget she's meant to see
about getting a bed for the night.

You see I'm worried that
she may have been hurried
and not made the booking.

I'm home? Don't need a reservation?
Have you got some confirmation?
Will you please just have a look?

No, I'm sure I have to book.
Must get a bed for tonight,
then I'll be alright...

I do not swear

I do not swear
Fuck
I do not swear
Fuck
I do not swear
Fuck, fuck
I have sworn
in sickness and in health
Fuck.

Respite at the garage

I want to wait.
Won't go to Tesco,
won't go and shop,
won't forget myself,
busy till I drop.
I want to sit and wait.

Warmth through the window,
encased in my chair,
music lulls, I can sit and stare.

Minutes pass, hovering, suspended.
I feel the pulse of time,
so precious in this life of mine.

Glad I have not yet forgotten
how to enter the moment
where I am not forgotten.

Bitch

Where the fuck have you gone, you bitch?
Rolled off my ship? Had your fill?
Come back, I need you here, you witch.

I toss, I fret, there's no off switch,
no one but you can fit the bill.
Come back, I need you here, you witch.

Adrift, with limbs and mind that twitch,
no soothing hand to hold them still.
Where the fuck have you gone, you bitch?

Is this the end, is this my ditch?
Not yet, I haven't had my fill.
Where the fuck have you gone, you bitch?
Come back, I need you here, you witch.

His anger

The gathering surprise of it,
the shock of rage
exploding domestic air.

Is this a gear change
or a smash up? Trailer
for the film to come?

Must focus now, be gentle,
allow the fury to subside
safely cushioned in my calm.

Concur, give some autonomy yet,
till words soft and worn will say
"Don't leave me, please don't go away."

Tea time

Four little squares of bread
      sitting on a plate.
One man of eighty-six
      getting in a state.
Toast spread with butter,
      oozing thick with jam,
man's all a flutter,
      he'll eat it if he can.

Questions come a plenty
      but answers there are few.
His mouth is here, the bread is there,
      between them what's to do?
No spoon, no fork or knife
      in sight to execute a plan,
there's something here that isn't right,
      he'll sort it if he can.

That woman, who might be his wife,
    is sitting there as well.
She doesn't see what's going on,
    he knows her, he can tell.
"What shall I do?" he blurts it out
    as shameful as it sounds,
for she might know and help him out;
    he waits while his heart pounds.

"Pick up the piece," she gently says,
    urging him to try.
Hesitant and fearful,
    he grips her with his eye.
Is this right, he wonders
    as fingers find the jam.
He's grateful for the help she gives,
    he'll tell her if he can.

Losing it

Words seize and shape my knowing,
keep it safe, weave meaning till voice,
the midwife of expression, lets fly.

Abruptly, threads split and fray.
Hydra filaments wave furiously,
failing to find words of similar complexion.

Careless tentacles connect by chance to
streams of otherness, unfamiliar, foreign
but good enough to carry voice.

Stumbling upon strands of anger,
shouting, swearing, making no sense,
I am lost. Help! Call the police! I need help!

Mutiny

He walks across the room
and stands stock still.
His face a mask, his eyes adrift.
No longer captain of his mind.

Words mutiny, abandon laws of syntax,
fret and froth with the spring tide,
revelling in their new freedom,
not content to follow his command.

The rope of meaning frayed,
the lanyard snapped,
the sail askew tearing in the wind
it drives him on, pitiless.

A soft moaning, hardly heard,
whispers to the wanton words
which, unheeding,
storm the spaces of his throat.

Lips and tongue thrust forth
on wings of breath
a message, meaningless
as the cry of gulls to human ear.

He will be heard

He is outraged, seething,
shaking, gut bleeding.
So much has been lost,
there's no counting the cost.
He will be heard.

He wants peace and solitude,
fuck unwanted platitudes.
He'll have no one in his house,
he'll stand firm against his spouse.
He will be heard.

With each snap inside his brain,
she's advanced on his terrain,
she has bled his own authority,
made her wish the main priority.
He will be heard.

He will show her his mettle.
No way will he settle
for half measures, or bin
the deep fury within.
He will be heard.

"Animale!" The wordy weapon flies,
resounds Wagnerian in its guise.
Releasing torrents of frustration,
breaching walls of indignation.
He will be heard.

She sits shocked, frozen,
as the venom unchosen
draws on the full weight
of his desperate state.
He will be heard.

His cruel word does not hide
the deep terror inside.
Deflating, she can guess
that she will acquiesce.
He will be heard.

And the glimmer of hope
to step off the tightrope
of tension and strain,
to feel more humane,
will not be heard.

Pick pick

Picking at my finger's skin
Pick pick
Delightfully rough and thin
Pick pick
Little pieces break and tear
Pick pick
Skin dust lying everywhere
Pick pick
Soon the blood begins to smear
Pick pick
Careful not to drop a tear
Pick pick
Grateful now the skin is peeled
Pick pick
There's a wound that can be healed
Pick pick.

Shadow lives

I tread a path not of my choosing
to shimmy with the shadow of his life
while mine steps lightly to one side.

I am vital to his well-being; worn smooth,
the rough edges of resentment
no longer catch on thorns of daily strife.

Sinking into the tick tock of his time
I settle for mysterious packages,
he will not open, arriving at the door.

The world is small and I devour
the foreign food of paint and ink, hungrily
kneading the clay which he disdains.

He dwells deep in crevasses of talent lost,
stretched like an elastic into the present.
Were it to ping, he'd surely die of shame.

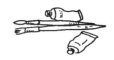

The corner of my quilt

Arriving at the corner of my quilt,
uncertain worlds beckon.
Flotsam and jetsam of time travelled,
the end of all my knowing.

Ice caps of certainty
shift, crack and shudder.
The anarchy of splintered thought
stirring ancient griefs and sorrows.

All is flux and floating.
An endless pull
in no particular direction; always
the fear of tumble, unable to return.

I clamber the angles of your terrain,
to remember the shape of my being,
to enquire into the seed of existence,
to be held captive, rooted and secure.

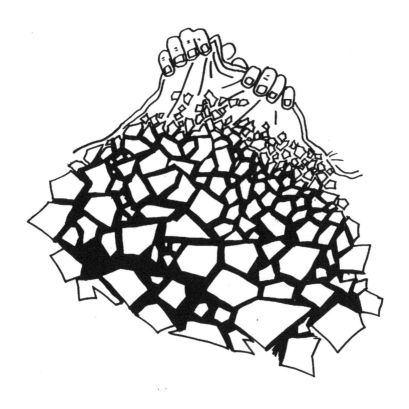

Cherries

You two women talk in smiles.
You say some more, it riles me
not to understand
what's going on.

You put bright cherries in my bowl.
I catch your hand to keep me whole,
to help me understand
what's going on.

You struggle but I hold you firm.
It's safer, though you twist and turn,
cos you won't say
what's going on.

Something's not right. I feel the rising fight in me
with the table tipping and water flying free.

You raise your voice; you scream you shout.
Ok, ok you want me out,
but tell me please,
what's going on?

I've found the sofa, sit and wait.
Kitchen's in an awful state.
I still don't know
what's going on.

It's quiet now, my fight has gone.
I wander back, there's something wrong.
"Want some cherries?"
Stupid question. Of course I do.

We eat, wash up; I feel deflated.
All I know is lost, outdated.
Just want to know
what's going on.

He peers around the corner

He peers around the corner, silent, unblinking, suspicious, assessing the moment to pounce, but without intention. Who am I now? He stares, motionless. A stranger to me. A stranger to himself.

We settle into dinner. He battles with balance of food on fork. Refusing spoon today, he staves off humiliation relenting only at the last hurdle, allowing me to gather stray morsels, shipwrecked across his plate, for the final push.

Painfully we arrive at fruit, peeled and presented in pieces which may or may not achieve the correct formation or have full authorisation to be scooped and stabbed for consumption. The journey is slow and I stop to wash and dry so that we arrive more or less together.

On this unusually balmy evening I invite him to the terrace. He watches me slip through the door and settle on the bench, then follows.

Inching towards the water butt, he pauses. Tentative fingers trace the rough surface finding lines to anchor into the present. Suddenly he looks up and with simple sincerity says, "I'm sorry for what's happening between us."

An unexpected gift springing from the tangle, speaks momentarily of love and is gone. He hovers, moves cautiously towards the bench, sits down. In our silence I hold his hand and the moment, precious.

Cracking up

For years thoughts were held secure,
catalogued with common logic.
Now a creaking, a cracking
of props which snap,
bring down the roof on reason.

Italian marble fractures.
Childhood marbles roll
and are lost.
Etna's lava bubbles
yeast, raising new worlds
where delusion bounces
into the harsh matter of fact.

Familiar eloquence dissolves
in a wash of fear rising, rising.
It is not a stab wound; it is a bruising.
It is not fatal; it is worse.

Daffodils

I look across the table
while sipping at my brew,
lives cut short before your time,
I am in awe of you.

Brave yellow trumpets
pushing through your green,
cut from your muddied field,
happy to be seen.

Proclaiming your beauty,
not loud but straight and true,
with dainty scent of promise
that winter's almost through.

You speak to me of courage
when fate tears life away
from paths that were expected
and you no longer have a say.

You tell me now's the moment
to grasp, to breathe, to shine.
However changed a life might be,
it's there to live, it's mine.

The unpaid carer's lot

A SHANTY - TO BE SUNG LUSTILY TO THE TUNE OF "BLOW THE MAN DOWN"

We are the carers we're stoic and strong
And it's wey hey, wearing us down
This is our story we'll sing you a song
Give us a break, it's wearing us down

CHORUS:
Come all you carers let's sing with one voice
And it's wey hey, wearing us down
Have to keep going we don't have a choice, hey!
Give us a break, it's wearing us down

True to our calling our loved ones come first
And it's wey hey, wearing us down
Sometimes it feels like a vessel will burst
Give us a break, it's wearing us down

We are the heroes who cook, clean and wash
And it's wey hey, wearing us down
Saving the government plenty of dosh
Give us a break, it's wearing us down

CHORUS:
Come all you carers let's sing with one voice
And it's wey hey, wearing us down
Have to keep going we don't have a choice, hey!
Give us a break, it's wearing us down

We have no handbook life's training is free
And it's wey hey, wearing us down
We're experts in nursing and psychology
Give us a break, it's wearing us down

Busy all day and we're up the night through
And it's wey hey, wearing us down
With fretting and wetting, what else can you do?
Give us a break, it's wearing us down

CHORUS:
Come all you carers let's sing with one voice
And it's wey hey, wearing us down
Have to keep going we don't have a choice, hey!
Give us a break, it's wearing us down

Sometimes it feels like our lives are in bits
And it's wey hey, wearing us down
Sometimes we're certainly losing our wits
Give us a break, it's wearing us down

Reason to moan and we've reason to shout
And it's wey hey, wearing us down
But God'll be dammed 'fore we let it out
Give us a break, it's wearing us down

CHORUS:
Come all you carers let's sing with one voice
And it's wey hey, wearing us down
Have to keep going we don't have a choice, hey!
Give us a break, it's wearing us down

Praise for us carers who work till we drop
And it's wey hey, wearing us down
Keeps us from dwelling on pain we can't stop
Give us a break, it's wearing us down

We are the carers we laugh and we sing
And it's wey hey, wearing us down
But don't be deceived cos it don't mean a thing
Give us a break, it's wearing us down

CHORUS:
We are the carers we sing with one voice
And it's wey hey, wearing us down
Have to keep going we don't have a choice, hey!
Give us a break, it's wearing us down

I AM INDEBTED...

to those who encouraged and supported me along the road to publication. Especially to Geri Dogmetchi, poet, gentle teacher and mentor, who saw some merit in my scribbles in the first place; to Shelagh Atkinson who was touched by the words and gave freely of her artistry; to fellow carer Jeanne Pring for her expertise, time and patience in developing the layout and dealing with all things technical, a true midwife of the project; to Jacqueline Graham for sharing her knowledge of publishing and signposting the way; to Lisa Rutter, founder of Dementia Club UK, and Mike Rich, CEO of Barnet Carers Trust, for supporting carers so they stay sane enough to express their creativity; to Emily Taylor from Arts4Dementia who responded unfailingly each time I reached out for ideas; to the anonymous donors who ensured the words got printed; to David Tims, musician supreme, who finds time to joyfully facilitate Singing for the Brain sessions on behalf of the Alzheimer's Society and whose penchant for sea shanties inspired my adaptation. And most importantly to my family, friends and fellow carers who had readings foisted upon them and whose positive feedback encouraged me to keep at it.

KARIN DE NOVELLIS

Over the years I have worked as a speech and language therapist, singer, teacher and counsellor, always preoccupied with the sharing of human experience through the spoken word. The worldwide pandemic and enforced isolation of lockdown led me to make connections in a different way. You hold the result in your hand. My husband is a Renaissance man. While he had a successful career in the world of finance, he could equally have become an opera singer, saxophonist, car mechanic, portrait painter, furniture restorer or composer. When dementia entered our home, so much was lost. The poems in this collection grew out of our shared experience of living with dementia. Profits from sales will be donated to charities supporting both people living with dementia and their unpaid carers.

SHELAGH ATKINSON

I grew up in Shropshire, studied Graphic Design at Camberwell School of Art. Travelled overland from London to India and ended up in Australia in the early 1970s. Worked as a Graphic Designer in Advertising agencies before running my own studio in Sydney. Currently retired with architect husband on the south coast of NSW at Mollymook. A dear mutual friend put me in touch with Karin.

"The reader gets a genuine and sincere insight into how dementia affects not just the person living with it but those living with us. The book as a whole did move me, it brought a lump to my throat but most important of all it made me think and reminded me that, whilst every person affected by dementia is unique and different, there are overlaps by way of the impact this wretched condition has on those closest to it."

KEITH OLIVER

Dementia ambassador and author of
Dear Alzheimer's: A Diary of Living with Dementia

"Most poetry is about youth – first kiss, first experience of love, being young and easy under the apple boughs. It is right that these first experiences are burned into our souls. But there is charm at every stage of life - even decrepitude, and these poems celebrate the precious beauty that comes with age and scream at you not to be profligate with your empathy. I enjoyed them very much."

JEREMY PAXMAN

Broadcaster, journalist and author

Lightning Source UK Ltd.
Milton Keynes UK
UKHW041822030922
408285UK00001B/84